private

aspen

private

modernism
in the mountains

helen thompson

photographs by **david marlow**

aspen

M

contents

5 aspen: landscape of desire

17 ■ gluck+
▲ preserving the land

33 ■ herbert bayer/fuse architecture & luis mendez architects
▲ aspen meadows townhouse

41 ■ studio b architecture + interiors
▲ along conundrum creek

53 ■ ellie brickham/rowland + broughton architecture and interior design
▲ a long view

65 ■ lake|flato architects
▲ true west

81 ■ s2 architects
▲ west end garden

91 ■ oppenheim architecture
▲ a dream fulfilled

103 ■ bohlin cywinski jackson
▲ modernist revival

115 ■ eigelberger architecture & design workshop
▲ in the valley

129 ■ gwathmey siegel & associates
▲ three trees

141 ■ ccy architects
▲ victorian music box

151 ■ s2 architects
▲ bayer redux

163 ■ eyrc architects
▲ inviting the light

171 ■ michael g. imber architects
▲ classical modernism

185 ■ herbert bayer/gilbert sanchez & jackie greenberg
▲ bayer legacy

197 ■ ccy architects
▲ building memories

211 ■ rowland + broughton architecture and interior design
▲ alpine influence

223 ■ zone 4 architects
▲ in the clouds

■ architects ▲ house

aspen

landscape of desire

Ansel Adams, *Maroon Bells, near Aspen, Colorado*

Plate 3 (detail) from Portfolio VI, 1951, printed 1974. Gelatin silver print, 7/110
Mildred Lane Kemper Art Museum, Washington University in St. Louis.
Gift of Sue and Paul Stohr, 2017.

The original tent housing the music festival was designed by Eero Saarinen in 1949. Herbert Bayer designed a replacement (left) in 1964.

Bayer's *Grass Mound*, a ring of molded earth enclosing a mound and a large native rock, was installed on the Aspen Institute campus in 1955, anticipating the Earth Art movement by almost twenty years.

Four Chromatic Gates, one in a series designed by Bayer, is installed in front of the Resnick Center for Herbert Bayer Studies on the Aspen Institute campus.

Aspen is a sensualist's paradise. You don't have to be in—or even near—this tiny Colorado mountain town to feel the power. It's an allure at odds with reality, though. Aspen is remote, often inaccessible, set amid inhospitable topography. The town is an anomaly of improbability, but the disconnect between reality and possibility hardly deters. Instead, it creates a dynamic on which residents and visitors thrive.

The geology is fierce in this remote pocket of the Rocky Mountains Sawatch Range. The western side of the massive swath of mountains feeds the headwaters of the Roaring Fork River and links with the Elk Mountains that ring the valley. Here the topography is exposed and charts a jagged profile that demands action.

The town is gripped on all sides by formidable mountains through which tempestuous creeks roar. Skies are implacably brooding before a big storm rumbles in or, when in the mood, they are ridiculously blue. Vegetation is lush in the summer; snow is sumptuous in the winter.

Aspen sits along the southeast end of the Roaring Fork Valley, with mountains and wilderness on three sides: Red Mountain to the north, Smuggler Mountain to the east, and Aspen Mountain to the south. These mountains are playgrounds for climbing, skiing, snowboarding, snow shoeing, and hiking in winter; hiking and camping in spring, summer, and fall. Rivers and creeks, engorged by runoff from the mountains, mean fishing, canoeing, kayaking, and rafting three seasons of the year. Aspen is undeniably enthralling—physically, philosophically, socially, culturally, and intellectually.

The splendor of nature abounds and has been much discussed. But I think there is a more revealing way to explain Aspen, and that is through its architecture. Aspen's evolution has both depended on architecture and has been expressed by architecture, a built world robustly responsive to the place in which it exists.

The surprise is that Aspen became a mecca for modernist architects—their admiration for the landscape and the freedom that Aspen represents has given us a fresh interpretation of how to live in a demanding landscape. Some houses offer respite; others an idiosyncratic spin on a personal vision; others luxuriate in their own glamour.

The development of modernism in Aspen occurred almost instantly—the joyful response to the horrors of a World War; the revelation that Colorado's ferocious landscape was an ideal setting for architectural experimentation; and the brave new ideas of Chicagoans Elizabeth and Walter Paepcke who saw possibility and pushed to make it real.

The first settlers were silver miners in the mid-1880s, who erected the most rudimentary kind of housing—tents. These adventurers soon elevated their accommodations to cabins along the main streets that were to become Aspen's downtown. Aspen was a boom town until the Panic of 1893; the next fifty years were "The Quiet Years" when the population dwindled to less than 1,000.

All of that changed when Walter Paepcke, founder of the Container Corporation of America, ventured into Aspen in the spring of 1945, urged by Elizabeth who had already visited the nearly deserted mining town. She recorded her first impression in a memoir: "At the top, we halted in frozen admiration. In all that landscape of rock, snow and ice, there was neither print of animal nor track of man. We were alone as though the world had just been created and we its first inhabitants."

To Walter Paepcke, Aspen was the idyllic location to create a place for a complete life with recreation, art, music, and education close at hand. His idea quickly took shape as the Aspen Institute of Humanistic Studies.

Before World War II, modernism was a European urban movement. Its luminaries were still in Europe, its most radical talents at the Bauhaus which was originally located in Weimar, Germany. The Bauhaus was to play a crucial role in Paepcke's Aspen plan. The school opened on April 1, 1919, fulfilling the vision of founding director Walter Gropius for a new model of education that united painting, sculpture, textiles, and architecture to produce buildings of the future. Twenty years later, when the school closed under Nazi pressure, Paepcke invited its past directors and teachers to come to Chicago. Mies van der Rohe accepted the industrialist's invitation to head the architecture department of Paepcke-funded Illinois Institute of Technology. IIT was considered the new outpost of the Bauhaus, where Mies had been the final director.

Paepcke was enthralled by modernism, and Chicago, still rebuilding after the fire of 1871, was an exciting place for artists, designers, and architects to be. The city was already a testing ground, starting with Louis Sullivan's seminal work in the 1890s. The strong horizontal lines of his apprentice Frank Loyd Wright's 1905 Unity Temple in Chicago presaged architecture of the future. Sullivan's dictum "Form ever follows function" is still the modernist's motto.

Chicago was nirvana for the visionary architect: steel could now be mass produced, a technological quantum leap that drove the production of skyscrapers from the mid-1880s on. Mies designed twenty of the buildings on the IIT campus, the greatest concentration of his buildings in the world, which includes his masterpiece, Crown Hall. Sleekly composed, the IIT campus elegantly expressed Mies's "less is more" approach.

Aspen became the unlikely portal through which many other German and Austrian designers passed. Its landscape was reminiscent of their homeland, and many were skiers. The idea of working, playing, and reinventing themselves was a magnetic draw. Not all fell under its spell, though: Walter Gropius declined Paepcke's invitation to help reinvent Aspen, but not before offering his now-famous advice: "Restore the best of the old, but if you build, build modern."

Undeterred, Paepcke sought out former Bauhaus master Herbert Bayer to oversee the design of the new Aspen campus. It turned out to be a fateful choice: the dashing 46-year-old Austrian epitomized Bauhaus concepts. Typographer, furniture designer, architect, and artist, Bayer was a generalist who was good at everything he did.

He was also prolific. Bayer redesigned several of the town's preeminent landmarks (the Hotel Jerome and the Opera House) and then set to work on the 40-acre campus of the Aspen Institute for Humanistic Studies, which includes the Aspen Institute, the Aspen Meadows Resort, the Aspen Music Festival and School, and the Aspen Center for Physics.

Paepcke had further thoughts. In the summer of 1949, Paepcke and Robert Hutchins, president of the University of Chicago, organized a Goethe Bicentennial celebration. They commissioned Finnish-American

Herbert Bayer in his studio, 1960.

The Aspen Art Museum, 2014, was designed by Shigeru Ban Architects in collaboration with Rowland + Broughton Architecture. The distinctive woven-wood panel facade, made of the composite material Prodema, allows light to filter into the space.

The legendary Hotel Jerome dates from 1889 and the Aspen silver boom. Rowland + Broughton completed a renovation and expansion in 2018.

The Resnick Center for Herbert Bayer Studies, designed by Jeffrey Berkus in collaboration with Rowland + Broughton, opened in 2022.

The Mollie hotel, designed by CCY Architects, anchors the corner of Garmisch and Main Streets, across from historic Paepcke Park. The brick base ties the building to the commercial center while wood siding above relates to the historic Victorian cottages of the West End.

The Mollie's interiors were designed by Post Company as an homage to Herbert Bayer and the Bauhaus. Post incorporated natural woods, leathers, earthen ceramics, and hand-dyed textiles as references to Aspen and the American West.

architect Eero Saarinen to design a vast white canvas tent under which lectures, discussions, and concerts could be enjoyed. The event spawned the Aspen Music Festival and School and the Aspen Institute, where participants could read and discuss writings by great thinkers. To accommodate guests, Bayer designed three flat-roofed guest chalets and a central building with a restaurant and offices. A year later came the Health Center, with its prismatic typographic entrance mural. Bayer completed the Walter Paepcke Memorial Building—which contains offices, a library, a gallery, and a 400-seat auditorium—in 1962. He also designed residences in and around Aspen, two of which are included here.

The Paepckes' exuberant and optimistic experiment took hold at the right time, in the right place, and with the right people. It got better over time, and a new architecture would also emerge that reflected the desire to honor the land, the sky, and the people in a way that had never happened before.

Some created an architectural statement that boldly addresses the dramatic topography; others were searching for a feeling, perhaps even a memory, and their houses—such as the house by CCY Architects that seems to have alighted in a sea of native grasses—almost erase themselves in deference to the natural world around them.

Other houses love the landscape so much they literally become a part of it. The two-part compound designed by Gluck+ Architects is a powerful demonstration of site-specific architecture. Just the opposite are the two beautifully renovated residences by Herbert Bayer. Both are unassuming and boxy. One gazes out on Hallam Lake and the other onto the grounds of the Aspen Institute, their forms never competing with the surrounding grandeur.

There is room in this complex landscape to explore other approaches. Complicated and exhilarating, the tripartite house by Charles Gwathmey foregrounds views from every angle and invites intellectual as well as sensual engagement between observer and the observed. And then there is a 1970s-era ski chalet renovated by Chad Oppenheim, who was lured back to Aspen by the memory of glittering holiday lights he first spied as a teenager. Oppenheim knew he wanted to live on Red Mountain, and decades later, he does.

Through these residences, we can clearly see how the idea of Aspen and the reality of Aspen are mutually invigorating. This little town deep in the Rockies is a place that activates every sense we have. It tells us what it is to feel alive. The first silver miners must have known it the minute they hoisted their picks over their shoulders; Elizabeth Paepcke felt it when she saw Aspen for the first time; the architects the Paepckes brought here understood it, too. And of course, visitors crave it—it's that feeling that has made Aspen so sought-after as a destination and a dazzling object of desire for so many people.

preserving the land

gluck+

There is abundant topography around Aspen—rushing rivers, looming mountains, rocky valleys cascading to dire vanishing points, and meadows wild with waving grasses. Residents are passionate about its beauty and about preserving it and some—such as the owners of this family compound designed by GLUCK+—go to great lengths to ensure that their dwelling doesn't impinge on the scenic splendor around it.

Peter Gluck has made known his views on the disconnect between architecture and environment. The architect has said that the houses his firm designs are correctives to the "megahouse" (the ones with pitched roofs and turrets, he specifies). Often the firm "mines" the building into the ground. The result is a non-building where very little shows except the landscape and amazing views. It was because of the modernist's no-nonsense opinion that an Aspen entrepreneur sought out Gluck and project architect Charlie Kaplan to design a multi-generational compound for his family in a narrow valley just outside town. There were compelling reasons to collaborate with Gluck, including the fact that he has a long history with Aspen, having designed and built three houses and a 14-unit affordable housing project there. Perhaps the most cogent reason, though, was Gluck's conviction that "a traditional house would destroy the landscape." His solution for the selvedge of property between a road and Castle Creek is an object lesson in the grace of site-specific architecture.

The project began as a main house, with the subsequent addition of a two-wing guest house. The two structures became case studies in architectural opposites. The main house came first—a two-story modernist glass, steel, and wood box that faces south toward Hayden Peak. It's sited to capture the sun and to collaborate with the river, an ever-moving force that enlivens the experience of being in the house.

The house feels as if it's floating above the landscape. Except for the entry enclosure that enfolds foyer, stairwell, and a powder room, the glass-encased first floor exists en plein air, transparent and revelatory: an open floor plan with living, dining, and kitchen spread out below the 10-foot-high ceiling supported by slender columns. Lightly poised over the soft, flat landscape, the house seems to allow the meadow to flow right through it. As prescribed by Corbusier in his *Five Points of Modernism*, there are roof gardens. Two meadows are forever in plain sight on the intersecting roofs of the guest house.

Perpendicular to the main house, and parallel to the road, one wing of the guest house integrates unconditionally with the rugged topography. One end of its roof rises out of the landscape in which the other end is literally immersed. It's a trajectory that passes over the other wing of the guest house, aiming straight at Hayden Peak. "We wanted to augment the view," Kaplan explains, "and we used the two roofs of the guest house as emphasis." The grassy flat roof of the guest house opposite the main house underscores the view, like a datum line; the ski-run roof emerges from the meadow at a trajectory that matches the angle of the slope of Mt. Hayden. From the vantage point of the interior courtyard, it's easy to visualize the impossible—stepping off the high end of the roof right onto Mt. Hayden's slopes (many miles away). Besides connecting an admirer to the far-away, the buildings create an immediate and intimate a liance. Together the two guest wings clasp the south end of an implied courtyard that unifies the three structures into a private family gathering place.

"We carved out the forest," says Gluck, "and we carved into the hill. The idea was to create a space so you can't see the house from the road and vice versa." At GLUCK+, architects manage design and construction in an integrated process that unites site and architecture. "We were trying to find a way to preserve the beautiful valley," says Gluck. Kaplan compares the operation to mining, digging into the hill to make a natural outcropping. "The plane the three structures are on is now 40 feet below the road," says Gluck. The effect is of three parallel universes—the public road; the river; and the meadow, each complementing the others.

Colorado topography is complicated. The architectural intervention in this family's little valley was also complicated, and the relationship between buildings and topography is elaborate in effort, but elegant in conclusion. For Gluck and Kaplan, there was only one acceptable result: "We wanted to leave the valley pretty much as it was," says Gluck. "The valley was beautiful then and it's beautiful now." ●

↑ In the main house, slender columns support the second floor, allowing unobstructed views. The open living space extends outside to a dining area overlooking Castle Creek.

→ A hallway extends from the entry into the heart of the house; the stair leads up to the second floor and a deck.

↑ A David Weeks Bottle Tiered Mobile hovers over the dining table in the main house. English sycamore and wenge are used for cabinetry in the kitchen and below the windows.

← [preceding pages] The intersecting bar forms of the guest house create an interior courtyard. The planes of the "roof meadow" render the house almost invisible from the road and highlight the original view from the main house.

↓ ↙ Together the main house and guest house form a private compound, sheltered by mountains and forest yet open to the sun and sky.

↙ The angle of the guest house roof is reflected in the upward slant of the ceiling and the widening clerestory windows, which follow the profile of the adjacent hillside.

↓ Glass doors in a corner bedroom in the guest house open to the lawn and pool; ipe wood screens filter out the sun and provide privacy as night. Clerestory windows give the impression that the grass-topped roof is floating above the room.

↓ Fully glazed walls in the living space of the guest house blur the boundary between inside and out.

aspen meadows townhouse

herbert bayer

⊕

fuse architecture & luis mendez architects

Ricki and John McHugh own an antiques store in downtown Aspen; they are admirers of the special, a predilection confirmed by their choice of residence. The couple occupies one of eight Herbert Bayer–designed townhouses sited across the street from the Aspen Institute. Built in the 1960s, the group was conceived by a modern art-loving triumvirate: fashion designer and modern art collector Larry Aldrich and the collector John Powers, and John Sarpa, a visionary developer.

At first, the three innovators worked with Bayer on their own two-story dwellings; Bayer designed five more, and a developer built an additional three twenty-five years later. Sarpa and his wife, Jan, still live in theirs and the McHughs are their neighbors—finally. Ricki had longed to live in one of the Bayer townhouses, a determination that was put to the test after she heard a rumor that one might come on the market. "It took ten years of negotiation before we finalized the sale," she explains.

The complex sits between two of Aspen's rushing waterways, Castle Creek and the mighty Roaring Fork River. Yet the buildings are characteristically unassuming, slipped between the white tree trunks of an aspen grove, their dark wood facades receding into the shadows and casting a spell of invisibility.

The McHugh townhouse needed comprehensive updating, executed within Aspen's preservation guidelines. The McHughs and Luis Menendez, a preservation architect, determined how extensive their proposed changes could be. Leaving the front of the building intact, the McHughs took the interior walls down to the studs, working with architect Jason La Pointe. The most significant decision was to expand the townhouse, pushing the back wall of the tiny, dark entry hall out three feet. This modest strategy yielded significant space: a powder room and a laundry room ramped up functionality; a bigger window brought in light and a bigger view. Existing windows in the living room were detailed with steel for a sleeker profile and brighter outlook.

Transparency was one of Ricki's space-enhancing strategies: all-glass railings along the upstairs landing replaced the wood balusters; they promote the feeling of being suspended midair above the living and dining room. The primary suite occupies the second floor, a secluded aerie that overlooks a garden island in front that belongs to the Aspen Institute and that Ricki (an avid gardener) tends as if it's her own. Tightly calibrated for efficiency and purpose, the townhouse purrs with clarity, a machine for living that's both minimal and flexible. The McHughs and La Pointe never veered from Bayer's original Bauhausian roots: clean lines, little or no decoration, and functional use of modern materials such as glass, concrete, and steel.

The McHughs live in a world comprehensively imagined by the Bauhaus master: civilization on one side, the natural environment on the other side. And, somehow, with Herbert Bayer as intercessor, these opposites are the unlikeliest of complements. ●

ALBERTO PINTO
VALLEY CURTAIN
GREAT MASTERS
VENETIAN CHIC
GREAT LODGES
THE LAST TWO MILLION

← *Blue Moon*, a painting by Herbert Bayer, hangs on the wall above shelving that displays a Bertoia bronze tree and other treasures. The Saarinen dining table is covered in shagreen.

↓ A 1950s-era pastel by Vicente Rojo is juxtaposed with a built-in display cabinet McHugh designed for objects collected on her travels.

↑
↖ Eighteenth-century topographical lithographs hang in the bathroom and over the bed in the primary bedroom. An eclectic group of ethnographic objects is displayed on the shelves.

studio b architecture + interiors

along conundrum creek

This charred-cedar-sided house—three rectangular boxes in syncopated alignment— sits in a triangular meadow with the avalanche-prone Aspen Mountain as its backdrop and the rowdy Conundrum Creek running beside it. Designed by architect Scott Lindenau of Studio B, the house possesses a mien of inscrutability and, at first glance, none of the transparency of modernist icons. Lindenau's glass house is here reinterpreted to suit the wild surroundings—from the front, the house is windowless, a bulwark to withstand nature's mighty forces. Not so from the back, which is all glass stretching from one side to the other, open to the abundance of the setting.

The house harmonizes with its natural surroundings with a profile that conforms to intricacies of the site. The plan was determined by the location's powerful features: one side is pushed back from the entry to allow for the bend in the creek; the other is pushed back even farther from the entry to edge out of the way of encroaching landscape. "The house," says Lindenau, "is bounded by a steep hill on one side and the river on the other. We inserted the house between them."

By fracturing the house into three parts to fit into the tight space, the architect maximized involvement in the terrain's diverse facets— view, river, trees, mountains, and light are all relished. It's almost too much, and Lindenau modulates the effect so that homeowners and guests are guided into the visual extravaganza from the front door and entry, where a glimpse of what is coming can be seen just above and around the entry hall wall and through a clerestory above it. Beyond the wall, the transparent great room delivers a seamless connection to the outdoors, offering stunning views from all sides. The drama comes into focus: the clerestory window emancipates the top slice of the panorama, tempering what might be overwhelming and making the fragment of the scene into a visual delicacy.

Other elements besides the dynamics of mountain and river challenged the architect: "The house is in a hollow," Lindenau says. Massive evergreens crowd into the narrow valley and tower over the property, casting it in moody shadow. Lindenau acknowledges the shadow, cloaking the house's three sections in near-black siding that merges with the overall gestalt. But the architect balanced the dark with its opposite. "I needed to get light inside the house," he says. To do so he literally raised the roof on the central section of the house—a shed roof (tilting at a barely perceptible 2.5 degree pitch to the south) appears to levitate over the structure's midsection, a modernist trope and also a graceful nod to the shed, the simplest of structures. Floating above the house as it does, the ever-so-slightly tilted roofline admits light and adds buoyancy.

In effect, the house becomes its own source of light—and for those inside watching the brooding drama outside, it's a sensation similar to basking inside the glow of a lantern. Light becomes an active participant day and night, a silent companion to the creek roaring past, the trees rustling in the wind, the bugling of moose and elk, and the long view of skiers zipping down Highland Mountain seven or so miles away. "This is an active site," says Linendau, "and nature is the priority. I almost wanted the house to disappear." ●

← [preceding pages] The charred-cedar-clad house is wedged into a hollow between Conundrum Creek and a steep hill. A stream from the creek flows into a natural pond that was enlarged as part of the project.

← The scored concrete approach cuts through the heavily wooded site in which the house almost disappears. The wall incorporates firewood storage.

↓ A series of landscape vignettes includes a path beside the stream and a picnic area at the edge of the meadow.

← Charred-cedar siding is almost indistinguishable amid the dappled shadows cast by the many fir trees.

→ ↘ The patio projects over the pool with the stream flowing underneath its edge, while the roof extends above to create a true outdoor living area.

↓ ↙ Fully glazed walls enclose the interior living spaces, where a neutral palette complements the greens and browns of the forest. Clerestory windows below a slightly raised shed roof admit light into the wood-paneled living room. White plaster walls in the adjacent kitchen add luminosity.

a long view

ellie brickham

⊕

rowland + broughton architecture and interior design

This house was designed in the 1960s by Ellie Brickham, Aspen's first female architect, for Nordic ski legend Stein Eriksen. Stretched out along a ridge, the lean modernist structure seems confidently reserved, an outlier in an environment that is so often hyperbolic.

Recently renovated by Rowland+Broughton, Ridge House sits at the end of a long driveway that wends its way through undulating terrain and a grove of aspens before reaching the gray sandstone building. The dwelling lies low to the ground, nuanced architecturally, thanks to the restraint inherent in Brickham's original design and in Sarah Broughton's respectful renovation. From the vantage point of the ridge, the residence gazes on Aspen five miles away.

Now home to a family of four, the steel, glass, and stone house is an observer, unobtrusive in the way that the best spectators always are. Precisely sited by Brickham to take the distant mountain drama into account, the building further benefits from Broughton's clarity of purpose: to open up the entire back of the building to the view. There's no missing the spectacle—spread out in view the moment the black steel-framed front doors are opened. The double-height living room—with its wall of glass—focuses on the panorama of Aspen's four ski mountains. Windows and the clerestory windows above them were added when the roof was raised during the renovation.

Broughton masterminded the transformation of the Brickham/Eriksen house, which had suffered from accretions of multiple additions. The renovation process was surgical—a painstaking excision of years' worth of layers that had accumulated on the walls, on the ceilings, on the roof, and even inside on some walls and a fireplace surround. "We were cracking open the house," says the current owner.

Inside Brickham had established a central spine for the house—an elegant north-to-south interior hallway onto which the rooms on both sides opened. Over the years, the hall had been modified with new walls that defined other spaces, compromising the spine so much that it lost structure and lucidity. "It was just a zig zag," the owner recalls. Broughton broadened and lengthened the hall so that the passage connects the children's wing at the north end to the primary suite at the south, 126 feet away. It's a journey that is enjoyed variously—the children speed from end to end, sometimes on scooters. The architect also enlarged doorways, removed walls between rooms, and moved rooms—the current kitchen replaced the original dining room and anchors the public space. "My clients wanted sight lines between the rooms," she says, "as well as better views of the landscape."

The hall has been transformed into a room itself—a gallery for the owners' art collection and a preamble to all the other rooms. Time and space became its most powerful features—passing through maximizes the pleasure of moving from one room to the next; each portal encourages stopping and looking. It's a ringside seat for the current owners who appreciate their role as spectators watching the clash of opposing weather systems or subtler natural phenomena such as rainbows, pink and blue clouds, and the moon rising over the mountains. The sense of place is extended into the landscape and beyond. That is the charismatic effect that architect Ellie Brickham attained with the original house, and it's the achievement of Sarah Broughton's liberating renovation. Both empowered the house to maximize one of the most elusive of architectural intangibles—space—which in Aspen is the ultimate luxury. ●

← [preceding pages] The back of the house is new construction clad in black metal siding with windows and doors framed in blackened steel.

↙ The charred-wood front door opens to a view across the living room to the mountains beyond. The entrance facade is clad in gray Appalachian sandstone.

↓ Clerestory windows, luminous plaster walls, and white oak floor and ceiling enhance the natural light in the living room. The painting is by Sarah Morris, a work from her *Pools* series

→ The fireplace in the primary bedroom, now updated with a honed limestone surround and steel chimney stack, is one of four that are original to the house.

↓ The generous hallway stretches from one end of the house to the other. Its walls are hung with a collection of contemporary paintings and works on paper.

▲ a long view ■ ellie brickham + rowland + broughton architecture and interior design

← ↙ The kitchen and casual dining area face the window wall and the views. Across the hall is the formal dining room, which overlooks the front of the house. It is generally used in the evening, unless one of the children has requisitioned the table for elaborate Lego constructions.

↓ In the primary suite, sliding glass doors open onto a deck and a view of Aspen's four ski mountains. A reading nook beside the fireplace is oriented to the view as well.

true west

lake | flato architects

Much of the eastern half of Colorado is part of the Great Plains, a 180-million-acre short and mid-grass prairie slicing through the middle of the United States. Some of its boundaries are nebulous and hard to pin down. But others—such as at Denver where the grasslands abruptly come to a stop and the blunt foothills of the Rockies encroach—are impressively obvious. Bits and pieces of these grasslands make appearances farther west in the Rockies, and in those places—including Aspen—the grassy lacunae are lovely interludes amid the bold-faced mountains.

"We always think of the land first," says Ted Flato, principal of Lake|Flato Architects. The firm has championed site-specific architecture for forty years, reframing conventional thought about the interdependence of land and the built environment.

Although the large landscape is ever-present here, it's at the perimeter, a fierce backdrop for a new house for an active family of six. In the midst of the rugged milieu, the property revealed a surprise: "This is a soft landscape," says Flato. The softness is undeniable, a remnant of the Great Plains, with two meadows—fluent with grasses in the summer and glittering with snow in the winter—that are a calm baseline for the brooding and jagged horizon. The tension between solid and evanescent is active. The mountains do not move, but the grasslands are always in motion, swaying in the wind and oblivious to gravity

"The site," says Flato, "floats out in the open landscape." It was oddly delicate in a landscape where fragility is not an advantage. Flato and the two project architects—Colin Gorsuch and Dan Carter—understood that this asset made the site special and designed a multi-functional house accordingly. It seems to float, too. Despite its size, the house appears to hover over the grassy plain, a glass-sided modernist pavilion linked on each end to a barn-sized gable reminiscent of structures built by the homesteaders who settled the Great Plains.

The tripartite house is sited obliquely to the street. Clad in vertical shou sugi ban planks, the building is formal, perhaps uncategorizable—it could have been scathed by a passing forest fire long ago or it could be an element of an agricultural relic. Whatever its provenance, the barn-like edifice looks clarified and irreplaceable, shielding the other two-thirds of the house from street view. "It steps down into the meadow in back," says Dan Carter, "so that it incorporates the landscape and doesn't overwhelm it."

At the north end, the owners' suite is a quiet and monolithic gable constructed with local field stone, cairn-like in its attention to domesticity and ancient in message. The suite is bracketed by two window walls; opposite the bed, the window overlooks a sea of grass, enticing an awakening sleeper to begin the day feeling as though they are immersed in a sea of grass. In between is a great room—where the kitchen, dining, and living areas combine forces. "The glass pavilion," says Gorsuch, "is set broadside toward the big meadow, which seems to spread into infinity in back." Its silhouette is modernist, but in function the transparent space is charmingly retrograde. Glamorous and glassy, this stretch of public space is basically a breezeway outfitted for year-round conviviality.

Transparency in this house is a counterpoint to solidity—the middle section is a sleek iteration of old-fashioned elements used for living comfortably outdoors. An open-air connecting hall was a strategy used by early pioneers; in the South and parts of the Southwest the dog-trot house served as both breezeway and conduit to channel cool air between two separate buildings. Meals were prepared and served there and sometimes a dog would trot through. Lake|Flato Architects reimagined a more luxe version for the Aspen house, but the connecting modernist glass link serves the same purpose as its predecessors as a place to cook, to have meals, and to relax.

Aside from practicalities, the transparent room's purpose is to foster a relationship with the outside. "It's a way to experience the meadow in all seasons," says Gorsuch. Experience comes in many forms. The room is the starting point for family excursions—summer and winter—onto the nearby Nordic trails for hiking. It is also a lyrically persuasive demonstration of the beauty of allowing a site to have its way. For Ted Flato, the significance of the glass pavilion extends far beyond the basics. It offers up a way to do the impossible—stop time. When we look at the meadow, we are looking into the here and now, and we are also locking into an iconic part of our shared history. "It's a view," says Ted Flato, "into the Great American West." ●

← [preceding pages] A boardwalk leads into an aspen grove and entry courtyard between two gabled pavilions, one clad in charred wood and the other in fieldstone.

→ A narrow concrete-slab pathway leads to the entry courtyard, a compressed approach to the expansive view of the mountains. A boulder marks the halfway point between the motor court and the front door.

→ A niche in the hallway between the public and private areas of the house is a place to work while contemplating the meadow and the mountains.

← Steel stairs with floating treads and a wire railing descend from the catwalk that connects the living space with the guest and common rooms. The walls are paneled in Douglas fir; the floors are concrete throughout.

↓ Transparency and solidity are in a dynamic relationship in the living room, where the glass walls expose nature and the beamed Douglas fir ceiling protects. The blackened-steel fireplace wall separates the space from the primary suite.

↓ The all-black kitchen glows in silvery morning light, a counterpoint to the blackened-steel fireplace wall at the other end of the expansive room.

↑ Stretching across the living space, the catwalk offers view of the landscape at either end.

→ [overleaf] The window walls of the living space reflect the meadow and aspen trees as a backdrop for the outdoor dining terrace.

s2 architects

west end garden

The West End of Aspen offers a concise survey of the town's residential architecture: miners' cabins and Victorian-era houses in original condition, renovated Victorian houses with additions, and modern designs coexist in the leafy, walkable idyll. And even though it's not obvious, the modern houses are Victorian sympathizers, thanks to the guidelines of the Aspen Historic Preservation Commission—and the panache with which architects apply those principles.

Debi and Jeff Wechsler, an NBA sports agent, already had a house in the West End and were in the habit of strolling their neighborhood. "I love looking at houses," Debi admits. Ultimately the couple purchased their favorite—a modern house designed by Aspen-based architect Joseph Spears. Boxy and two stories, with another floor below grade, the dwelling reflects the International Style that Herbert Bayer used for his buildings at the Aspen Institute. Spears specified a white limestone for the first level; the top floor is clad in narrow vertical strips of ash wood, with a notable interruption. At the streetside corners, widely spaced slats cover two porch-sized inset windows upstairs. On the ground level, the corresponding corner receives the same treatment, but the glass front door makes it clear that this is the entry. Rather than looking as if it has set itself down resolutely on a corner lot, the house radiates stylish inscrutabilty.

The house is in scale with its Victorian neighbors, and it is composed of materials that are consonant with other styles in Aspen. Turn the wood slats on their sides and they are a svelte rendition of clapboard siding seen throughout the West End. The enclosed entry is a modern version of a porch, facing the street with a setback aligning with other houses on the street—all keeping the neighborhood feeling pedestrian friendly.

Inside, the two-story stairwell feels like an open-air structure, with gaps between the two-inch wood slats and sky visible through them. Light streams in from the upper level, which also frames a mountain view, plus clouds. Luminous spaces elsewhere come to mind: Christ in the Desert Monastery in Abiqui, New Mexico, with its two-story double-paned bay windows and Thorncrown Chapel in Eureka Springs, Arkansas, with its 425 windows and exposed structure.

To the left of the airy entry is a loft-like space for kitchen, dining, and living areas. A wall of steel-framed glass sliding doors yields to the outside counterpart—a covered terrace with cooking, dining, and living. Beyond is beautiful garden that fills the adjacent lot acquired by the previous owners.

Under the guidance of landscape architect Monique Spears, the original owners, and subsequently the Wechslers, transformed the space into a wonderland of shady glamour. Low limestone walls topped with black steel planters frame the grassy field that's lush with blue, purple, and white flowers—black snake root with its showy white spires; double white peonies, allium with its ornamental purple pompom blooms, white royal wedding poppies, and the leafy green petticoats of hosta spill over the planters—a profusion that has earned the neighborhood nickname "The Park."

The city of Aspen manages more than thirty parks, ranging from neighborhood playgrounds to vast open spaces with mountain vistas. The Wechslers' yard, at the intersection of two streets, attracts many passersby in its unofficial capacity as a park. Just as it delighted the Wechslers as they walked the West End, the resplendent garden now gives pleasure to others strolling by, living proof of why people who moved to Aspen for the skiing have stayed for the summers. ●

← [preceding pages] Slatted cedar siding on the street facades filters light and adds privacy; the limestone panels allude to Herbert Bayer's white buildings on the Aspen Institute campus.

← Floating white oak treads on the stairway appear to be suspended in the double-height entry space; the glass panels supporting the railing reinforce the overall transparency of the room.

↓ The slatted facade wraps around the public spaces like a screen and connects visually to the cedar ceiling. The fireplace surround is clad in limestone blocks in a running bond pattern; floors are black Conte basalt. Elmwood cabinetwork is installed below the windows.

↖ A low wall of coarse textured limestone encloses the backyard, allowing passersby a view of the garden. Hosta and ferns are a dense ground cover; allium thrives with its purple pompom blooms along with lady's mantle and snakeroot.

↑ A wall of sliding glass doors connects the indoor and outdoor living spaces. Tent-like triangular panels protect the patio.

a dream fulfilled

oppenheim architecture

Architect Chad Oppenheim first visited Aspen on a Christmas ski trip with his parents when he was 15. He immediately knew that he wanted to live in the then-quirky ski town where the notorious journalist and candidate for sheriff Hunter S. Thompson cavorted. Specifically, the teenage Oppenheim wanted a house on Red Mountain, at the time a cozy enclave a few twists and turns above the town's West End.

In 2008 the adult Oppenheim, now married with two children, discovered a modest 1970s-era ski chalet, distressed after a bevy of haphazard renovations by previous owners. It sits on a quarter acre of land with a stream percolating along the nether reaches of the property. And it is on Red Mountain, now an exclusive neighborhood. Aspen Mountain is directly across, the base terminating at Aspen's premier shopping district. Its ski run is a jagged white scar in the winter that dominates the view from most of the rooms in the house.

The ski chalet today—after an extensive stripping down and regrooming—is much the same in both form and function, if not in aesthetics. The tower-like house, with its rooms stacked to accommodate the steep slope, was a dizzying 1970s time capsule where a blue aluminum roof seemed to have alighted. Built around flights of stairs embedded in the center of the structure, the walk-out basement—with a massive fireplace and pool table—has direct access to a garden that eases down to the merry little stream. On the middle level, another fireplace anchors a wall with seating on either side; a dining space and Oppenheim's study around the corner open onto a tiny courtyard on one side and to the garden on the other. Wall-size windows face Aspen Mountain across a wraparound terrace. The kitchen is up a short flight of stairs that overlooks the space. Up another flight of steps are the children's bedrooms, and at the top is the owners' suite, snugly nested under the gabled roof that frames the view of the mountain.

Oppenheim brought order to the multilevel madness with a restricted palette of neutral colors and an unorthodox range of textural materials that enrich the house with nuance. He stripped off the exterior facade—a pastiche of stucco and wood siding—and wrapped the exterior with salvaged barn wood; to imply the interchangeability of inside and outside, the interior walls are also salvaged barn wood. The blue roof is now dark copper. The haunches of the house are clad in hunks of granite, fostering the impression that the house has decided to emerge intact from the granitic landscape and allow people to come inside to live. "I didn't want the house to look like architecture," Oppenheim says. "I wanted to capture a feeling."

Feelings, though, can be elusive—if not crushed—in this Rocky Mountain stronghold, where the surrounding summits are citadels and the weather is a mendacious captor, enticing but also dangerous. It is challenging to stand up to that kind of visual and meteorological brutality, especially if capturing an emotion is the goal. And yet Oppenheim has skillfully done just that with this house; a contrarian approach that adroitly sidesteps the seemingly ubiquitous local manifesto to respond in kind to the geologic melodrama. "I actually wanted the house to disappear," says the architect. Nothing in Oppenheim's architecture competes with the landscape—in fact, if there were a way for architecture to be liminal, barely perceptible as if hovering over a sensory threshold, this house has found it. In the summer, the rock-and-wood-clad house is of a piece with the grassy slope it sits on. In the winter the house recedes—especially during a snowfall—making it it seem as if it has slipped into a niche between the snowflakes, minimal, softly colored, and beguiling. ●

→ Floors in the dining room are salvaged barn wood, which is also used to clad the house. A wall hanging of living moss is an earthy contrast to the sophisticated plaster walls behind it.

↓ The living room fireplace is original to the house, but it is now fabricated in steel. A salvaged barn wood partition separates the space from the kitchen. A textural wall hanging is the companion to the living moss wall hanging in the dining room.

→ [overleaf] The study was originally a greenhouse that was incorporated into the renovation. Black plaster walls add textural softness to the surrounding structural steel beams; sliding glass doors lead to the deck.

MICRO:ART
HANDBOOK OF NATURE STUDY
THE ELECTRIC STATE
THE HIDDEN LIFE AROUND US
CHARLES WHITE
HOMMAGE
Atlas of Digital Architecture
The Story of Aspen
THE LAND IN BETWEEN
A MAN & HIS CAR
SEEING SILENCE
AFRO SURF
MUSEUM BHAVAN
Canon

← *The Silent Valley*, a photograph by Chinese artist Yang Yongliang, hangs in the entry under wood beams retained from the original house. A charred-wood bench is beneath.

↓ Windows, such as this slit-like aperture in the primary bath, frame views across the valley to Aspen Mountain and focus on nearby trees to connect the viewer to the landscape.

↑ A black wall in the study contrasts with the whites in the living room. A step up defines the spaces.

↑ Kitchen cabinets, seating, and walls are made of salvaged barn wood. Floors are slate slabs, their heft matched by the wooden beams anchored to the ceiling with steel plates. The door opens onto the deck.

← The grays of the salvaged barn wood cladding are at one with a brooding sky. Glass railings enclose a granite ledge with outdoor seating.

→ In the primary suite, a pair of chairs is strategically placed in a window niche with an expansive view of the valley, Aspen Highlands, and Maroon Bells.

bohlin cywinski jackson

modernist revival

Mountains, sky, weather, and snow announce themselves forcefully in Colorado, but from a more intimate vantage point, that elemental world seems quiet, textural, less colorful, softer. That is the architectural lesson proffered by a stone, glass, and wood structure stretched between two knolls and immersed in the inner life of a dramatic natural setting. The house was designed by Bohlin Cywinski Jackson, a firm with a revelatory, deeply investigative design process that culminates in buildings whose existence seems inevitable.

The property is unique, the site of the only Aspen project by pioneering modernist Marcel Breuer. He designed the original house in 1949 while he was teaching at the Harvard Graduate School of Design, a commission arranged by his Bauhaus colleague and Aspen resident Herbert Bayer. The first owner was not satisfied with some aspects of the house, and a lawsuit ensued. The second owner then neglected the house, and at some point, its linearity was obscured by a coat of pink paint (perhaps a tribute, however awkward, to the bright pink Herbert Bayer painted Aspen philanthropists Walter and Elizabeth Paepcke's West End residence). The current owner and his wife purchased the property in 2004 and lived in it for two years before concluding the deteriorating structure was unsalvageable.

"We had lived there long enough to get a sense of the space, the light, and the setting," the husband explains. Those elements represented the spirit of the house, and the couple began a search for an architect who could rethink the package of enticing assets and whose work aligned with the wife's modernist sensibilities.

The couple's criteria fit only one person—Peter Bohlin, recognized for his ability to understand environments, particularly those whose credibility had been lost or overlooked, and to revive them with modernistic clarity. The couple paired BCJ with New York–based architect and interior designer Lee Mindel of SheltonMindel, who composed the furniture plan and worked closely with Bohlin and BCJ partner Ray Calabro on interior finishes, furniture, and other details.

Bohlin and Calabro inserted the house between the two knolls of the original Breuer site. "It ended up being within a half of a degree of the Breuer footprint," notes the husband. The tightly framed view in the first-floor entry opens up on the glazed wall on the second floor—a panorama of the adjacent meadow and the 245-acre North Star Nature Preserve, home to the Roaring Fork River, lush wetlands, and an elk migration corridor. Then there is the staggering sweep of snowcapped peaks in the distance. It's a spectacle, determining not just materials for the house but also the interiors and finishes. "There is a softness and a hardness to the design, just like the landscape," Mindel says, referring to the shapely furniture he selected as well as the natural textural palette.

The lower portion of exterior is clad in split-faced Valser quartzite—a glittering metamorphic rock Bohlin, Calabro, and their clients selected on site at a Swiss quarry. Horizontal mahogany and cedar panels confer privacy to the second floor—except for a narrow window that allows a tantalizing view through the house and into the sky beyond. Three freestanding quartzite walls extend from the front of the house through to the back and out to the meadow. They insert themselves into the topography and become part of it. "The walls root you in the landscape," Calabro says. "The house seems to stretch and fold into the terrain and moves beyond the idea of architecture as mere enclosure."

Where the walls anchor, other strategies liberate. A wall of stained cedar originating in the forecourt slices through the ground floor and terminates in the tall grass in the back. An interior quartzite wall opposite the cedar wall cuts upward through to the living room, where it becomes the chimney piece. A staircase with a glass railing rises from the entry to the elegant pavilion-like space.

Peter Bohlin likes to say that his architecture has a sense of inevitability: it is what it should be. Bohlin, Calabro, and their colleagues examine every possibility and all the alternatives, and then they consider again. The rightness of the solution is sensed, felt, desired, and loved. The house between two knolls tacitly summons the family hither—husband, wife, children, and grandchildren. "Everyone," says Ray Calabro, "wants to be there." ●

← [preceding pages] Quartzite walls extend from the house, grounding it in the landscape. Above, the plaster of the broad overhang extends into the living room achieving the effect of a continuous ceiling inside and out.

← The quartzite wall is part of the double-height entry and frames an enfilade of spaces that extends the width of the house. Overhead, a plaster ceiling also directs the view through the house.

↓ A quartzite chimney wall defines one end of the living space, with a reading alcove tucked alongside. Bespoke furniture, textiles, and floor coverings—including cashmere-soft carpets by V'Soske and low-key modern classics by Poul Kjærholm, Ward Bennett, and Jean Prouvé—create an air of subdued yet sumptuous minimalism.

← Walnut floors in a hall off the entry complement the cantilevered walnut treads of the floating glass-paneled staircase, which is set in front of a double-height wall of black-stained cedar boards.

→ The double-height entry extends through the house. Hallways on the upper floor face each other across the space.

↖ The sleeping niche in the primary bedroom is framed in wood: walnut floor, Douglas fir wall panel and ceiling, and exterior mahogany panels that extend into a glassed-in workspace. A photograph by Edward Burtynsky hangs beside the bed.

↑ The main floor is unified by a ceiling defined by Douglas fir beams and walnut floors; glass walls and sliding doors give the open-plan area the feeling of a modernist pavilion.

in the valley

eigelberger architecture & design workshop

Set deep within a narrow valley carved out by glaciers 20,000 years ago, this property follows the upper shelf of Castle Creek. Most recently, the natural clearing in a dense forest of aspens, fir, and spruce was part of a ranch—the well-worn two-track ranch road, paddocks, and original fencing were still there when the owners purchased the property. Also still in place was a wooden platform, the unofficial destination for skiers on the double black diamond runs on Highland Bowl. From this vantage point, the terrain unfolds, revealing views of Castle Creek and Aspen Mountain to the east, Highlands Ski Resort to the west, the town of Aspen to the north, and Hayden Road to the south.

The isolation appealed to the owners. For architect Christof Eigelberger and landscape architect Mike Albert, both committed to holistic architecture and landscape design, the site was an opportunity to explore inclusive views of architecture. "Architecture and landscape should work together to form meaningful exterior spaces that are equal to each other," says Eigelberger.

Part summer camp, part modernist elegy, the glass, bark-shingle, and native-stone buildings—two rectangular boxes—are perpendicular to each other. Connecting architecture to nature, they open up to the views like a seam inserted into the landscape to keep nature uninterrupted. "We left everything as it was and made transition spaces into the man-made," Eigelberger says.

A stone slab approach to the front door begins the entry procession to the public rooms of the house. On the way the path transects a front courtyard and enacts the connection between the wild and the cultivated—separated physically but allied visually. To the right, Mike Albert built a low stone wall to frame the existing aspen trees, animated by light flickering through the canopy overhead. To the left, he designed a more formal grid of ash trees with an understory of ferns that references Colorado's Late Cretaceous swampy history.

Just ahead, the glass-and-steel gridded front door and window wall are visual transition elements, the transparent preface to the living room. Sliding glass doors open to an expansive terrace that edges into the restored wildflower meadow; the meadow, luxurious as a plush carpet, unfurls into the awaiting aspen forest. Towering aspens perfectly frame a view of Mt. Hayden, on which Albert and Eigelberger centered the living room. The immediacy of the terrace and the view ignite a rush of awareness of just how fluid the engagement between natural and man-made is here. The primary suite, to the right of the living room, extends out from the house, piercing the enveloping forest.

Another breezeway bisects the second wing of the house. There is also a view here, but a tight one—a concise section, a snapshot of aspen trunks, its graphic intimacy the antithesis of the expansive view from the living space. This framed view is the terminus of a 900-foot approach to the house from the main road.

"We wanted to hold the house as far back from the road as possible," says Mike Albert, "so that the drive marks the entrance not just to the property but to the house." The terrain is undulating, but neither designer wanted to interfere with its natural slope. Instead, the new serpentine drive gracefully negotiates the vertical change, following the land's contours, passing within a foot or two of some trees as it meanders through the forest where some aspens soar to more than 70 feet tall. "It's magical," says Albert. "It makes it feel like the road has been there all along and the trees grew up around it." The designers made the most of the road's rural personality, reinforcing it with an application of recycled asphalt. The crunchy sound tires make as they roll over the surface is an essential part of the textural psychology choreographed by architect and landscape architect.

The experience is immersive, a slow descent into a realm where forest, house, and the spaces between exist in harmony. "It looks like the house was lowered into the landscape," says Albert. The richly textural exterior—poplar bark siding that is variously gray green to light brown and copper roof shingles that patinate with time—allows the house to evolve organically in concert with the landscape. Materials are the connective tissue between interior, building, and landscape, an eloquent relationship that preserves the serenity of the unique site. ●

← Curved spouts keep an eighteenth-century French trough bubbling with water next to a stacked stone wall bordering the entry walk. The wall separates the uncultivated part of the landscaping and the more formal area around the courtyard.

↓ To keep the existing aspen forest intact, the approach road winds through the trees and follows the contours of the land as it descends to the house.

WOLF
WOLF

← The kitchen wall is composed of copper shingles intended to oxidize over time. The glazed tile of the backsplash contrasts in scale and finish. Floors throughout are reclaimed white oak.

↓ Living areas inside and out merge in this house; the patio's irregular borders further blur the distinction between the natural and the man-made.

↖ A rough-sawn Alaskan white cedar peaked ceiling in the primary bedroom is a visual connection to the deeply wooded site. The room is a walk-out, with seamless access to the outside via glass sliding doors.

↑ Although the form of this house is modernist, natural materials—such as the chunky native rock walls seen in the dining room—ground the building in the surrounding terrain.

↑ Transparency and solidity are in tension in this house with views through the steel-framed front door and the entry hall into the meadow and forest behind the house.

↗ The transition from the dining room to the terrace is uninterrupted, thanks to pocketing sliding glass doors. Copper shingles on the roof will patinate over time.

↓ Long stone walls draw a viewer's gaze into the farthest reaches of the landscape, from terrace to meadow, to the forest, and finally to Hayden Peak in the distance.

↓ A glazed link connects the kitchen to the garage, another transparent moment in the house.

↑ In the primary bathroom, the architect took the idea of forest bathing literally, punching out a steel-framed glass nook directly into the wooded landscape.

← Purple cone flowers flourish next to the aspen trees on the terrace.

gwathmey siegel & associates

three trees

This concrete, marble, steel, and glass house claims its place on a steep slope on the side of Shadow Mountain, a prominent location in Aspen with 360-degree views. In some places, the multipartite residence appears to burrow into the granitic hillside much the way that an Italian hillside town attaches to the terrain.

The house is the fullest expression of what can liberate architecture when a three-dimensional approach isn't enough. In this case the late Charles Gwathmey relied on an extra-pliant fourth dimension—time—to pick up the slack, propelling the architectural narrative into an experience that proceeds through time and space, and ideally also through the owner's imagination. "Charlie," says the owner, "is talking to us through this house."

Three Trees is the firm's only Colorado project, and it was the last house designed by Gwathmey before his death in 2009. Associate partner Dirk Kramer guided the project to completion. It's hard to look at this unapologetically dynamic house and not think about Gwathmey's very first architectural idea, the house he designed for his parents in Amagansett, New York. A self-contained cedar-sided modernist puzzle with a curved half-stairwell at the front of the building, that house is disarmingly simple on the outside and extremely intricate inside.

Gwathmey's fascination with curved elements is evident in both his first and his last houses—his commitment to the rigor of modernism is imposingly present in Three Trees, but the architect knew there was more, and promoted it. "This is a very dynamic house," says the owner. "There is nothing static about it." The contrast between exterior and interior makes for a sensual duality offered exclusively to those who enter.

There are three floors in this complicated residence, some overlapping, others tantalizing with glimpses of spaces beyond. "As you proceed through the house," says Kramer, "there is an experiential change than makes you want to keep going—a resolution of intersections and spaces—that is emotionally satisfying."

Entry is via a single glass-and-steel door; two similarly sized windows stacked above the door offer a tantalizing view into the upper reaches of the light-filled foyer from the outside. There, on the right, a double-height wall is the moment for theatricality—major art is displayed there, setting a high bar for the rest of the owners' contemporary art placed on the walls, on the floors, and hanging from ceilings throughout the house.

A glass staircase promises both subtlety and spectacle, not so different from each other. As each nuance accumulates, the overall effect becomes spectacle. The glamorous transparent staircase is the starting point of the public space, which is marshalled at the second-level landing. There is much information presented—and none of it all at once. Much, though, is sensed, and the architecture practically insists that you trust your senses. "Our client was fanatical about getting light into the house," says Kramer. "This house is about many things, but most of all it's about light." Here light is seen, unseen, and sensed—but that is exactly the point.

Light is a prized commodity in Aspen, where the mountains obscure the sun starting at about 4 p.m. on a winter's afternoon. Even if each of the three pavilions has its own vantage point and exposure to natural light, the architects responded to the owner's admitted fanaticism about natural light with their own fanaticism. There are many versions of natural light, it turns out, and all are celebrated here.

In front of the second-level landing, an opaque glass floor offers a sumptuous glow on the way to the dining room. At night, the celestial experience is replaced with the glitzy, intensified by the reflection bouncing off a mirrored cocktail bar inset in the wall of the hallway. Guests are also aware of light is coming in elsewhere—the source turns out to be the monumental, mullioned window in the double-height living room, which overlooks a woodland scene.

"Light activates the spaces," says Kramer. "You want to walk through it, as if you are being pulled through to the end of the hall." And no wonder—three porthole-like floor apertures (also serving as skylights for the pool below) are enticing, programmed to change colors (pink, purple, or blue). The window wall in the dining room opens to a meticulously curated terrace and garden embedded into the mountain's edge. The immense power of the mountains is a counterpoint to the phenomenon of transparency and weightlessness that comes with Gwathmey's reckoning with light.

The third level feels sacrosanct, far removed from the two floors below. A central aisle overlooks the living room, the mullioned window commanding attention. The floor is home to two studies, a guest bedroom, and the owners' suite, which opens to a terrace above the courtyard and pool.

It is possible to conclude that when Gwathmey designed Three Trees (which ended up being his ultimate house in more ways than one), he was doing something besides encouraging an examination of a specific house or of architectural aspirations in general. The architect's idea was to lay out an opportunity for the right client to explore themselves. Not just once, either, but all the time. "I never get tired of it," says the owner. "This house interacts with you. It gets into your head. You feel it." ●

← [preceding pages] The house, composed of three pavilions, is embedded in a hillside overlooking Aspen.

← Double-height divided windows in the living room look onto a lawn as precisely groomed as the architecture. Artwork on display includes a sculpture by Rachel Harrison and a painting by Rudolf Stingel.

↓ Behind the living room is a passage to the dining room with a glowing opaque glass floor and a mirrored cabinet that also serves as the bar.

← The gallery's luminous plaster tilting wall functions as an avalanche wall as well as a backdrop for works by Mike Kelley Richard Artschwanger, Rachel Harrison, Rashid Johnson, and Harold Ancart.

→ The first-floor swimming pool is a dazzling respite, lit by three skylights in changing hues ranging from blue to pink to purple.

↑ The family room offers casual dining just off the kitchen and overlooks the terrace. An Alex Israel *Self-Portrait* hangs above the sofa, with a sculpture by Mark Grotjahn beside it. On the wall is a vacuum-formed polystyrene bomber jacket by Seth Price.

← The formal dining room displays works by Sigmar Polke, Jeff Koons, Jacqueline Humphries, Carol Bove, and Walead Beshty.

ccy architects

victorian music box

The architectural language of Aspen began austerely—tents were housing for seven silver prospectors camping near the confluence of the Roaring Fork River and Castle Creek in 1879. By 1883 silver mining was a prodigious moneymaker, and miners' cabins were a practical and more comfortable solution for the influx of hopefuls. Simple wooden dwellings with gable roofs rose in and around Aspen, often constructed according to store-bought plans.

Established as a hub for silver mining, Aspen developed infrastructure and amenities—an opera house, a fancy hotel (The Jerome), a streetcar system, two banks, and six newspapers—for its 12,000 residents. Modest mining cabins were revamped with Victorian flourishes, while genuine Victorian residences, garnished with gingerbread, also shouldered their way in, symbols of new-found—if illusory—stability.

These early cabins and Victorian cottages now constitute an Aspen vernacular architecture. Especially prized are those that retain their original architectural integrity; for an arts-loving couple, that kind of authenticity held irresistible allure. They had been looking for a permanent home in Aspen for years, a search that wasn't burdened by the typical considerations of style, size, or age. The relaxed agenda allowed a deliberate version of house-hunting that eventually succeeded because the husband walked every street in Aspen—fortunately a small and walkable town.

His reconnaissance yielded three possible houses, although none was for sale. One—a Victorian—was deliciously inconsistent with the couple's classical tastes, but its powerful provenance tempted. The winsome house was all charm, with a front porch, peaked roof, and double-hung windows that looked out on the neighborhood park, property originally owned by Aspen Institute founder Walter Paepcke.

The house had been turned into a duplex with a large, clumsy addition, but the best thing about the miner's cabin-turned-Victorian was that it occupied a triple lot. The couple negotiated the purchase of both the Victorian and the duplex addition and then turned to CCY Architects to reimagine the landmark. The new version would accommodate guests, children, grandchildren, guest artists, and especially music recitals—some magic would also have to play a part so that these aspirations wouldn't overwhelm the 1880s structure.

The duplex addition had one redeeming value: it had no historic significance, which meant that it could be demolished. The Aspen Historic Preservation Committee approved a small, detached guest house on the second lot—a charismatic alter ego to its Victorian sibling, proposed by CCY partner John Cottle.

"It was a way to respect the spirit of the neighborhood and the historic Victorian, but with a contemporary dimension," says Cottle. The spirit is palpable: pianist Artur Rubenstein, physicist Albert Einstein, and Aspen philanthropist Paepcke convened in the living room to discuss ideas that evolved into the Aspen Institute. "This house had so much potential to respect Aspen's history and also to support a way to live in the twenty-first century," says the wife. "It's a crucial link to the downtown tapestry."

In legend, the trim Victorian lived large. In actuality, it was 1,600 square feet. There were, though, ways to make it feel bigger even if it couldn't be bigger: open up the spaces, streamline the sightlines, and bring the outdoors in. Inside, the house would become a subtly streamlined modernist version of its former self, with Victorian detailing on the meticulously restored exterior, as required by the preservation committee.

The new guest house and recital space—called the Music Box—forms a courtyard with the Victorian. It was an elegant arrangement that created a private interior patio, but it meant, too, that the new gabled structure was exposed on two sides on one of Aspen's most prominent street corners. Privacy was topic A between the clients and their architects.

Cottle and project architect Evan Barrett concocted an inspired solution: a perforated Galvalume siding that wraps the two public facades of the Music Box. The pattern of the perforations, based on Chopin's Nocturne in E-flat Major, Op. 9, No. 2, is superimposed on the front of the building as if it were a gigantic piece of sheet music. "It's a design that reflects the power of music to move you beyond language into a universal experience," the wife says. On the interior, the recital space and stairwell are filled with dappled light that moves through the space in ever-changing configurations. And the patterned siding is even more alluring at night when the interior light twinkles through the perforations.

Often the couple heads out toward music—"We are close to the Music Tent," says the wife, referring to the tent designed in 1949 by Eero Saarinen, an allusion to the significance of tents in Aspen. That tent was replaced by a seasonal structure designed by Herbert Bayer in 1964, which, in turn, was replaced in 2000 with a permanent building by Aspen architect Harry Teague. Because Aspen is easily navigated on foot, the pair walks to performances by some of the world's greatest musical artists, one of whom might even be staying in the Music Box and practicing pre-recital scales on the resident Steinway grand piano. ●

← Butting front windows are a signal that the new guest house and performance studio next to the Victorian main house is a modern reinterpretation of the Aspen vernacular. The use of similar materials—metal roofing and metal reverse batten siding—helps to establish the connection.

→ The guest house sits at a 90-degree angle to the original house, creating a patio connecting the two buildings. The musical pattern used on the front of the new building reappears on the side of the garage.

→ [overleaf] The living room in the guest house is used for performances. The pattern of the exterior screen is visible through the windows. The triptych on the end wall is a digital composition by Isabel LeMay.

← A metal staircase with perforated treads serves as both a lightwell and passage between the three floors of the house. The pendants are etched-glass teardrops hanging from woven brass mesh.

→ Doorways in the Victorian house were widened and sightlines established for a modern, streamlined attitude. The dining room opens onto the courtyard and the guest house.

↓ The original front door is still in place (as required by the Historic Preservation Commission) and just visible from the living room. Interior doors were replaced with sleeker versions.

bayer redux

s2 architects

Jamie and Margo Koval share a deep connection to Aspen. Originally from Chicago, Jamie's family began skiing in Aspen in the late 1950s and owned several properties in town. It was their love for the outdoors, the sense of community, and the fact that it was a historic town that drew them here. Since then, Aspen has been a constant presence in their lives.

Both Jamie and Margo have an appreciation for midcentury modern design. Jamie, trained as a graphic designer, has a particular admiration for the Bauhaus movement. In 2017 the couple were fortunate to find a vacant house for sale in East Aspen, situated on a small wooded lot less than a mile from downtown. Having spent years building and renovating properties, they were drawn to the idea of creating a modern home that would complement the site and resonate with the architectural elements they loved in Aspen. The property was on the market for just a day before the Kovals purchased it, sight unseen.

They hired architect Joseph Spears to design the house, a decision based on his reputation for crafting modern homes with a focus on both aesthetics and clarity. For inspiration, the Kovals shared several places they admired with Spears. The journey began with the Farnsworth House, an elegant floating glass structure designed by Mies van der Rohe. The conversation then shifted to the Hotel Jerome and the Aspen Art Museum, designed by Shigeru Ban, both admired for their purity of form and timeless appeal. Finally, they spoke about one of their favorite places: the Aspen Meadows and Aspen Institute campus, designed by Herbert Bayer in the West End.

For both the Kovals and their architect, these shared references formed a universal language. "Jamie has a precise eye," says Spears. "He was very specific about what he wanted his house to be." The new home would face the mountains from within a grove of aspens, pines, spruces, and shrub oaks. Despite the steep slope, the architect and clients saw the potential to site the house on a flat expanse that sat parallel to the street, allowing the building to hover above the slope. Everyone was excited by the idea of a pure rectangular form.

This form has a philosophical connection to Bayer's work. Long and lean, the building thrives on the dynamic between solidity and transparency. The materials and color palette are restrained—glass, concrete, steel, black, white, and walnut. Both ends of the house are wrapped in hemlock wood, providing a natural separation between the kitchen and garage on one side and the entry and owners' suite on the other. In between, expansive glass walls float freely, unencumbered by visible support structures. The wood and glass elements are set within a crisp white plaster shell, a clear nod to midcentury architecture with a foundation of Bauhaus-inspired earthiness.

The house holds a secret revealed only upon entering: a lower floor is tucked beneath the double-height entry. A floating walkway spans the stairwell, a glass railing on one side and a floor to ceiling window on the other, connecting the public space with the owners' suite, while framing the mountain view. Downstairs, three bedrooms and a media room open onto a patio that extends to the surrounding landscape.

Spears has firmly grounded the house in its environment, merging one end into the knoll upon which it sits. The connection between the house, the site, and the outdoors is seamless. "The house emerges out of the hill," says Spears. "It's a nod to Bayer and his landforms." He is referencing Bayer's *Earth Mound* (1954) at the Aspen Institute, a pioneering work that predated the Earth Art movement of the 1960s and '70s. Bayer's forward-thinking vision set the stage for what remains modern today, demonstrating an imagination that continues to inspire.

After the completion of the house, the Kovals found an image of the Aspen residence and studio Bayer built for himself. Much to their surprise, the design of the house was long, minimal, glass and rectangular, perched on a small lot on Red Mountain: beautiful in its stature and surprisingly familiar. ●

← [preceding pages] Solidity and transparency interact, with both ends of the house wrapped in hemlock wood and wall-size panes of glass in between. A white plaster shell encloses the exterior, merging International Style architecture with midcentury warmth.

↑ ←

The entrance is at the end of the path, sheltered by a wide overhang. Hemlock walls at both ends extend to the interior, blurring the distinction between inside and out.

↓
↙

Airy interior spaces are energized by intentionally close views of the landscape, such as the scrim of aspen trees at the front of the house. Walnut cabinets topped with a black quartzite counter create a strong datum line below the ever-changing scenery.
In the kitchen, white Corian and walnut cabinetwork extend the materials palette of the house.

↑ A ground-floor workspace is inserted underneath the floating staircase that descends from the entry.

↑ The primary bedroom looks through windows directly into the trees; a black steel fireplace is inset into walnut cabinetry at the foot of the bed.

→ The double-height entry hall slices through the house, separating public and private spaces. A ten-light bronze chandelier illuminates the stairwell.

→ A black steel pivot door opens onto the entry hall where Oscar Lakeman's *Container #101* hangs over a built-in bench. A grid of concrete pavers extends throughout the house.

eyrc architects

inviting the light

A two-story modernist house is adroitly sited in Aspen's historic West End, a contrarian in a neighborhood where most of the houses—ornate Victorians—could seem giddy in comparison. Instead, the two-story basalt, wood, blackened steel, and glass house has taken its place in a longer train of architectural thought. Designed by Takashi Yanai, a partner in Los Angeles–based EYRC Architects, the juxtaposition of seeming opposites was motivational: "The house has a dialogue with the old Victorians," Yanai says.

Houses in this venerable neighborhood focus on a triangular shaped park. Yanai's modernist house savors what it sees, its mostly glass front gazing directly into a dense grove of towering fir trees that mass around the park's perimeter. The scene is particular and immediate: the fir needles quiver in the summer breeze; the branches sag with snow in the winter.

The owners are long-time clients of EYRC. Yanai had previously designed a house for them in a similarly walkable urban neighborhood in Palo Alto, California. The couple gravitated to Aspen's West End because the close-knit environments were akin. "They loved the familiar residential scale of the Aspen neighborhood," says Yanai.

It is a setting familiar to the architect—his firm is proficient in building on open or underused urban land. And, the Aspen site had its delights: "We liked the challenge of the infill lot," he explains. "Plus, we had nature to work with." The two advantages attracted Yanai, but they didn't work to mutual benefit. To open up the house to nature, it would have to be exposed to neighbors on all sides—not to mention the many patrons of the park across the street.

Counterintuitively, Yanai designed a surprisingly transparent house—glass on all sides, interrupted by intervals of solidity. From the park the stylish house looks like two boxes stacked on top of two more boxes, intersecting and overlapping.

The residence is situated on a strong north–south axis that engages with the park and offers sweeping views of Aspen Mountain behind. It is the most charismatic of vantage points, a dynamic available only to those inside the house. The mountain's active social and botanical life is visible, even from a distance. In the summer the slope is lush with wildflowers; in the fall, the aspens turn gold; in the winter skiers zip down its snowy veneer.

Despite all the activity in front and back, the house is solidly reserved. Massive rectangular chunks of rough, split-faced basalt clad most of the ground floor, with a wide rectangular window wall left of the front door that exposes the living and dining area, and a tall slender rectangle of a window on the right that slices into the kitchen.

In Aspen proper, land on which to build is limited. New residences usually have a level below grade, as does this one. But land scarcity is merely a physical limitation and not an aesthetic one, with the result that stairwells here have reached an art form. "The triple-height stairwell," Yanai notes, "is a sculpture, a key moment in the house." With black steel panel railings on one side and a perforated screen from ground level to the upper floor on the other, the contrast between delicate and solid is ever present. The enveloping screen provides privacy on the sides of the house, and at the same time, filters light throughout the upper floors of the compact dwelling.

Yanai has honored other architectural elements historically present in Aspen: a path leads from street to front door, a canopy covers the entry, windows face the street, and materials—especially the upper floor's board and batten siding—adhere to the local vernacular. The basalt exterior evokes the region's mining history. But the architect's discourse pushes for more depth and breadth than what's obvious. "I wanted to add another layer of awareness," he says, "to bring a new dimension to the West End."

The fact that both the Victorians and the rock-clad house survive the contrast is the starting point of a richly provocative demonstration of how to explore the gray areas of opposing ideas. With this house, Yanai proposes a way to see a relationship that was always there but that would have escaped both notice and imagination if Yanai had not provided a way to experience it. ●

↑ A desk and cabinets are built into the blackened-steel panels of the stairwell.

↑ Concrete walls, Vals Stone slab floors, and white oak cabinetry create a neutral setting for *After Redon (The Seashell)* by Mary Weatherford.

→ The triple-height stairwell is a sculptural element composed of torqued steel panels and contrasting floating Vals Stone treads.

→ A perforated screen wraps around steel-framed glazing on two sides of the house, admitting light in a pattern that references the dappled light filtering through the aspen trees surrounding the house.

→ [overleaf] The split-face basalt cladding used on the exterior extends into the ground-floor living area. *Super Group, 2017* by Richard Prince hangs to the left of the window; *Seascape True Colors* by Rashid Johnson is installed above the sofa.

KROMSON

classical modernism

michael g. imber architects

Plato knew it all along—the cube is primordial; math, geology, and physics now confirm that the cube is the average shape of all rocks. The philosopher's theory of inherent shape has recently been confirmed by geologists, but it was understood instinctively by the earliest home builders thousands of years ago as well as by the keenest modernists.

And so, up a mysterious winding dirt road and across a valley from the Elk Mountains, a concrete house composed of three cubic pavilions does not seem at all out of place. On the contrary, the structures sit elegantly next to a gravel motor court, enclosed by aspen groves above Castle Creek. The hipped rooflines of the pavilions, designed by architect Michael Imber, crisply respond to the three rugged summits of Hayden Peak on the horizon beyond. Brooding and capped with snow, the summits are the jagged antithesis of the concrete pavilions, which seem to be custodians of the grassy plateau.

The pavilions also obscure the view an arriving guest would savor of Hayden Peak, a special request of the owner—an arts patron and rancher with an instinct for delayed gratification. She knew that the spectacular view should be incrementally delivered from inside the house. "The trick," says Imber, "is how you bring someone through it and get them to pause before they arrive at the entire view."

According to the owner, the reveal had to start at the ground level as the visitor descends four steps from the foyer to living room: first, the pool and terrace come into view; then, farther inward, the meadow beyond the pool makes an appearance; arrival at the living room—the heart of the house. The room frames the multidimensional universe of formidable mountains, brilliant blue sky, and poofy clouds powerfully enough to bring an observer to a complete standstill in front of the view.

The owner intended to share this view with the many guests who come for parties or for weekends, and the house is designed with that in mind. Two guest suites, with sitting areas and generous bathrooms, anchor opposite ends of the house. One looks out on Hayden Peak, the other onto a secluded pond down the slope from the house. The living and dining rooms are the solid middle ground—one space that includes the kitchen and dining area and then opens out onto the terrace. Sixteen-foot ceilings cap expansive walls that display the owner's impressive modern art collection. The gallery is bathed in natural light and glorified by the room's lush materiality, an ideal space for viewing the art and for getting comfortable with it.

The monumental setting is the darker complement of an equation solved by the house—despite its refined solidity the boxy residence achieves the effect of being lighter than air. "That's because the polished concrete sides encapsulate the room's light and space," says the architect. His is a convincing explanation for the way luminosity activates a space so that it seems ultra-dimensional. Although the owner is an ardent admirer of modernism, she went the other way for her own house, choosing Imber, who is well known as a classicist. Imber's interpretations of historical styles (Spanish, French, coastal, Texas vernacular, and Greek Revival) unerringly embody all that is subjective about occupying a house.

The impetus for the choice had a sentimental dimension as well. Looking through Imber's 2002 monograph *Ranches, Villas, and Houses*, she was shocked to see her childhood home in the book. Imber explained that he had designed a replacement for that house, which had burned in the mid-1990s. For her, Imber's new design captured the essence of the long-vanished home. "It was exactly like I remembered it when I was a child," she says.

The notion of house as holder and shaper of emotions is basic to everything Imber designs, and he deftly shifted his aesthetic from classical to modern. "It isn't that difficult for a classicist to design modern," he says, noting the classical hipped roofs atop each boxy pavilion in the Aspen residence. "The principles of proportion, light, materiality, and sequences of space are the important elements no matter what." ●

← [preceding pages] The rear facade is fully glazed to take advantage of a spectacular view of Hayden Peak.

← →

Framed views, both large and small, predominate in this house. Majestic fir trees bordering the motor court are seen through the front door, while an aspen grove and secluded pond beckon from one of the guest bedrooms.

← [preceding pages] The living room is centered on the magnificent panorama of Hayden Peak, a view that defines the house. The reflective surface of the polished steel framing is intended to enhance the view.

→ A light-based work by Mads Christensen glows in the subdued light of the foyer, which is paneled in white oak.

↓ Modernist icons—Brno dining chairs and Saarinen Tulip side chairs—are ready for guests in the living and dining area. Works by Donald Sultan, Tom Wesselman, James Turrell, and Harland Miller hang on the floating art wall.

← An Alexander Calder mobile hangs from the living room ceiling. Barcelona chairs and Milo Baughman rounded-back sofas for Thayer Coggin sit on a honeycomb-patterned hide rug.

↓ William Nelson's *Marilyn and the Egg Man* hangs above the bed in one of the guestrooms.

bayer legacy

herbert bayer

⊕

gilbert sanchez & jackie greenberg

Herbert Bayer shaped the visual identity of Aspen—he designed houses and buildings in Aspen between 1946 and 1965, and he left an architectural heritage that has quietly defined the town into the present. A former director of the Bauhaus, Bayer endorsed a holistic approach to integrated design: art, architecture, mind, body, and landscape were all one, each complementing the others; each reinforcing the others. This residence is within a few blocks of the Aspen Institute and embodies Bayer's belief system. Painted a soft gray color, the unimposing house recedes from the street into a grove of towering aspens. Its reticence, though, comes with a challenge. The limestone-block path from the street aims directly into the house, piercing the volume created by the front courtyard and confident that all who follow it will want to go inside.

And that is what happened more than twenty-five years ago to the current owners of this modest lakeside villa. "The minute I walked down the path into the courtyard," says one of the owners, "I could see through the sliding glass doors through the living room and through the other glass doors down to Hallam Lake, and my heart started bumping."

Interiors designed according to Bauhaus principles are subordinate to the relationship of the house to the site. Here, the low roof, the many windows, the neutral colors all defer to the mountains in the distance. The ceilings seemed unusually low to the prospective buyers. "They were less than eight feet," recalls the lanky husband. "But my wife loved the house, and we bought it. That's the only reason to buy something."

The house was in original—if terrible—shape, which included the absence of kitchen cabinets. But Jackie Greenberg, one of the owners' daughters, who had just graduated from architecture school, wanted to take the house on as a project. "Bayer's aesthetic was mine then," she says. "And it still is."

As a first step, she approached the Aspen Historic Preservation Commission about adding a garage with a bedroom and an office above. Her parents needed more space, but they also wanted to maintain Bayer's design. The conflicting goals were unexpectedly resolved in adhering to the mandate of the Preservation Commission that the street front of the house could not change, and any additions must be clearly legible. The expansion stayed within the language of Bauhaus design with a subtle difference between old and new. The house is the original gray, and the two-story addition is just a few breaths darker. The result is a seamless integration of old and new.

In developing the design, the daughter collaborated with architect Gilbert Sanchez, an ardent modernist and a skilled researcher. He found Bayer's drawings and a set of construction documents in the Herbert Bayer Archives at the Denver Art Museum. More significantly, there were also drawings for a proposed addition in which Bayer expanded the owners' suite—"Exactly as we ended up doing," Sanchez says. But there was no suggestion of adding a second story.

Sanchez responded with a bold solution: an elliptical double-height stairwell at the rear of the residence. Tall multipaned windows usher in light that activates the entire house with energy; more light glimmers through clerestory windows encircling the cornice like a halo. Sanchez justified inserting the graceful geometry into the boxy profile of the house because other modernists had embraced curved forms. It also gently distinguishes old from new on the exterior.

"The shape," says the daughter, "was also in Bayer's repertoire, especially in his *World Geographic Atlas*." The book, published in 1953, was commissioned by the Container Corporation of America and became a landmark graphic design and data visualization.

As their research confirmed, the modification was still within the language Bayer consistently relied on. "I felt at home making an intervention on it," says the daughter. It took only one night for her father to be won over by the totality of the experience: "When I woke up after my first night there, the sun was shining off the lake—it was dazzling." He fell in love with the house, but it's possible he had no choice. "The house," says his wife, "made him fall in love with it."

The stairwell invigorated the house architecturally, ensuring the survival of the modernist house—one of only three Bayer-designed residences still extant in Aspen. As an example of Bayer's philosophy, the house is a testament to the durability of Bauhaus ideals and to Bayer's aesthetic vision for the future of a town he shaped so indelibly. ●

← [preceding pages] The house overlooks a nature preserve (donated in 1968 by Elizabeth Paepcke) and Hallam Lake through an expansive glass window wall and clerestory windows added in the renovation. KAWS' *Chum* wall hanging is an energetic muse; the lamp is by Giacometti.

← The house is clad in stucco in the original light gray, as mandated by the Historic Preservation Commission. The limestone block path into the entry is original as is the open beamed overhang above the entry sequence and courtyard.

↓ The window wall and clerestory extend to the bedrooms at the back of the house, which also look out onto the nature preserve and Hallam Lake. The table lamp is by Giacometti.

← The elliptical, double-height addition provides access to the new second floor and brings copious natural light into the house.

→ Alexander Calder's painted metal sculpture *Jeune Fille et Sa Suite* is installed in front of the double-height wall of mullioned windows. Thanks to open treads, the stair does not obstruct the view.

→ [overleaf] "Topiary" table and chairs by Knoll enliven the terrace overlooking Hallam Lake.

ccy architects

building memories

There is a rustle of memory that lingers over this stone, wood, and glass house designed by Rich Carr, Todd Kennedy, and Gage Reese of CCY Architects. Long and low with the bearing of a base camp, the residence is a series of three discrete volumes. All are linked under the stretch of a shed roof angled to follow the upward drift of the site in the Roaring Fork Valley, just northwest of downtown Aspen. Clad in vertical slats of weathered cedar, the house seems to withdraw into the landscape—in the summer, into a field of natural grasses and in the winter behind a scrim of snow.

The house is oriented on an east–west axis, with views of Garrett Peak and the pastoral Snowmass Creek Valley to the south. And, although it's not obvious, the Continental Divide slides through the Elk Mountains to the southwest. To find the ideal site on which to build, the design team spent two days walking the property, noting that there was a peculiar bipartite component to the alternatingly rocky-then-lush terrain.

A natural clearing between six spruce trees was the reward for the search. It offered the best views and also promised privacy, shielding the house in the grove that stood at a natural demarcation between ecosystems—on one side was the high desert with sage, brush, and scrub oaks; on the other side, with the spruces, a subalpine ecology. The house was sited on that fracture—neatly slotted into the embrace of the old growth spruces.

"There are two different experiences in this house," says the husband, a native of Norway. "If you look south you see a cold snowy climate. If you look north, there can be piles of snow, but it's warm on the patio." The house is one room deep, with a long hallway extending from the left of the entry to the dining, kitchen, and guest rooms. It's also on that side that the house hovers over the sloping landscape, with two bedrooms sheltered under two first-floor bedrooms. When the couple is alone in the house, they can close off the wing. On the other side of the living area, and up a few steps, is the owners' suite. "We wanted the house to feel intimate, like a cabin, when we are alone there," says the wife, "but it also accommodates family when they come to visit."

The house was inspired by the husband's multigenerational family compound near Morgedal, Norway, where he and his family spend part of each year. "Aspen grew on me," he says. "There are incredible opportunities to be outside to ski, hike, bike, and fish."

Being outdoors is essential for the entire family. The architects designed the house to be used as a base for both cross-country and downhill skiing—and then they pulled it apart for multi-tasking. At the far end, the owners' suite stands on its own—bookended by two transparent connections: a covered but wall-less passageway separating it from the sauna; and the living room, which behaves as a porch with expansive glass doors front and back—open-air, casual, welcoming both nature and people. "The house erases itself," says Rich Carr. It's as if the house is in a perpetual dialogue with nature, one that invites the homeowners to join in. "When I'm inside I always feel like I'm outside," says the wife. "When I'm outside, the inside is right there." ●

← [preceding pages] In summer, the house emerges from a field of natural grasses and low shrubs.

← →

Exterior passages with natural stone pavers are protected by oak overhangs. Panels of horizontal black siding mark the entry and surround the built-in wood storage.

← [preceding pages] The tension between the bold horizontal form and the vertical weathered cedar siding gives the house a sculptural presence in the landscape.

→ The same materials—weathered cedar slats, native rock, black siding, concrete, and oak—are featured in the interiors of the house to layer together the experience of being in the natural site and in the building simultaneously.

↓ Black is used to dramatic effect: a blackened steel sliding door conceals fireplace and firewood and the black siding wall above conceals the primary suite.

→ In the primary suite, the black siding wall displays framed botanical specimens the husband made as a youth in Norway. The entire room is clad in tone-on-tone white oak for a refined demeanor.

↓ Tone-on-tone white oak also defines the kitchen where it is used for walls and ceiling, as well as the millwork and built-in furniture. The iron chandelier was designed by CCY architect Gage Reese.

alpine influence

rowland + broughton architecture and interior design

There's a soulful alliance between the Austrian Alps and the Rockies that has connected the two regions since World War II, when the U.S. Army 10th Mountain Division trained in and near Aspen. The kinship still holds charm, as it did for the owner of this house designed by Sarah Broughton of Rowland + Broughton Architects.

The two-story structure sits in a meadow carved out by glaciers as they ground through the Roaring Fork Valley. The owner had lived and worked in Austria, and she was profoundly influenced by the mountains, the meadows, and especially by the wooden Alpine huts strategically sited for the views and an overnight respite.

"I learned to appreciate organic materials in Austria," she says. "All the huts with wood floors and ceilings were bringing nature inside." Nature plays a dual role in the owner's psyche because she also associates it with memories of coziness. Austrians call it *Gemutlicheit*, a word that conveys the feeling of friendliness and good cheer. The benevolent recollection spills over into memories of her mother, who loved being in nature and marveled at even its most basic attributes. On the other hand, though, nature isn't always cozy; it encompasses a larger reality—whether it's the Alps or the Rockies—that can be daunting.

Counterintuitively, this Aspen residence responds to these opposites by being both open to the world and cozily intimate. The glass, shou sugi ban, and metal house straddles both worlds, fusing intimacy with exposure, two opposites that are difficult to reconcile. In evoking a gabled farmhouse, Broughton is referencing the area's agricultural history, but she has imagined an idiosyncratic expression—a gabled farmhouse that's mostly glass. With a reassuringly iconic profile, the house occupies its place with pristine serenity, a jewel box miraculously intact on the edge of a meadow and in the middle of the wild.

The owner wanted the logical floorplan that a two-story house offers. "I like verticality," she says. "It's a good way to separate public and private spaces." On the first floor, a generous entry hall merges with the living room to the right; the kitchen is adjacent, with a book-lined dining room beyond; the owner's office is tucked behind. A wraparound terrace extends the living spaces and then merges into the meadow. Upstairs are the owner's suite, children's bedrooms, and a craft room.

Silhouette was as important as function for the owner, and the L shape appealed, another insight from her light-loving mother. "She instilled in me the value of a southern exposure," the owner explains. "With the L shape comes both the sunrise and the sunset." The plan also offered wind protection and established an axis that is optimal for solar gain.

Broughton elaborated further: the downstairs living room and the upstairs common area each bump out a few feet, a deviation from the L to a squared-off D shape that admits light on three sides of the rooms and into the rest of the house. White plaster walls and Austrian spruce plank floors and ceilings magnify the luminosity.

The house is the design descendant of sturdy agricultural buildings. "But it does something delicate," says Broughton. The owner experiences the house as a respite, an oasis where she can regroup. "The landscape is aggressive," the architect says, "but she views it from her edge of the meadow." It's a perspective that the owner appreciates compositionally, as if it were art. "There is a very clear foreground, middle ground, and background," she says. Not to mention all the wildlife that makes its way through this natural sequence: elk migrating summer and winter, bobcats, deer, and mountain lions.

The owner shares the property with her former husband, whose house is within walking, biking, hiking, or snow-shoeing distance. The couple's children and family dogs have easy access to both houses and both parents. "When we split up," the owner says, "we went through all the possibilities of how a family could live and decided to build a second house for me on the property. We're proud of our solution." To Broughton, this kind of out-of-the-box thinking that energizes her clients is what happens in Aspen. "People are looking for something when they come here," she says. "We are a community of outliers choosing different priorities." The topography has a lot to do with it, its grandeur liberating courageous thinking and generating a sense of peace is its own reward. Aspenites know the feeling. "Every morning when I wake up," says the owner, "my view is of Mt. Hayden. It's heavenly here and you can't help but be grateful." ●

→ The house sits on the edge of a meadow, part of a former agricultural area, which the owner experiences as an oasis in the rugged landscape beyond.

↓ The architecture references the agricultural history: a gabled farmhouse with cedar siding accented by Cameron ledge stone, charred-wood screens, and metal-clad windows.

← [preceding pages] The living room projects slightly from the main block of the house to capture both sunrise and sunset. Scrub oak trees immediately outside the window and the field beyond mitigate the power of the mountains.

← In the entry, a steel staircase with open Austrian spruce treads complements the darker charred-wood screens on the exterior. Both the floors and the ceiling are also Austrian spruce.

↓ A shapely double fireplace by the Haas Brothers serves both the living room and the small den tucked behind it. The fireplace surround was hand-carved in Portugal in Pele de Tigre marble. Above it, *More Solitude* glows in LED script.

↑ Austrian spruce floors and ceilings continue throughout the first floor and into the kitchen where a marble island doubles as a serving station for events. Beyond is the dining room/library, which is illuminated by a vintage Murano glass chandelier.

↑ → The primary suite on the second floor features a bedroom and deck looking out to Mt. Hayden and an airy bathroom with a vintage clawfoot tub.

→ A private sculptural spiral stair connects the primary suite to the owner's office on the first floor.

in the clouds

zone 4 architects

"It's like living in a cloud," says one of the owners of this house, which backs up to Red Butte and offers open views toward Independence Pass through a glass facade. Designed by Bill Pollock of Zone 4 Architects, the building sits on a plateau that dips down eighty feet into Maroon Creek, which then joins up with the Roaring Fork River. The owners both grew up within miles of each other near Aspen, and they have a lot of experience with clouds, the frothy hosts filled with water droplets and ice crystals that routinely mound up against the mountains encircling the town.

The cloud reference is apt: stretches of atmospheric gray of the exterior and the diaphanous interiors of whites, beiges, and grays orchestrated by Studio Piet Boon create a palette that suits during Aspen's eight snowy months each year. The colors seem disembodied, an airiness that infuses the space with a sense of being aloft.

"I am admirer of Le Corbusier," says Pollock. He was thinking of the Swiss-French architect's concept of a "box in the air" when he designed this Aspen house—stacking three rectilinear volumes with a fourth overlapping the bottom two volumes, a symmetrically dimensional response to the rugged profile of the mountains. A guest house is behind the primary suite, an aerie slotted into place by itself above the two lower floors. The house is geometrically executed, urging dynamic interaction between the solid walls that set boundaries and the glass walls that open up the margins.

Entry is on the second (ground) level, which is shielded by a series of four walls that extend across the length of the house. They add privacy, but not too much. Windows in different sizes and shapes—a Morse code of dots, dashes, and spaces—create a sequence that controls how light comes into the house. Two sidelights flank the front door, illuminating the entry and the stairs. Luminous plaster walls and ceilings throughout the house gleam, a sympathetic mix of reflection and atmosphere.

This is a house distinguished by its own window language: a clerestory, window walls, and vertical slits on the front side are a preamble to the fully exposed backside of the house, which reveals an inexhaustible view and all that happens there. Pollock has made it easy—the family simply steps out into nature from the lowest level's covered lounge area into their backyard which opens onto trails for hiking, running, cross-country and downhill skiing, horseback riding, and birding.

There is quite a bit more that goes on in this couple's backyard, and it's been happening for centuries. "We are in the elk migration corridor," the wife says. Every fall and every spring thousands of female elk, their calves, and bulls—descendants of Eurasian ancestors that migrated across the Bering Land Bridge to North America 12,000 years ago—process single file across the Roaring Fork Valley. They disperse for days to graze; their bugling—a high-pitched squeal signaling to potential female mates—is an eerie soundtrack to the majestic seasonal odyssey. A sight such as this one has been recurring for thousands of years, but for first-timers enchantment overrides all else: "Our children thought they were seeing Santa's reindeer," says the wife.

The couple envisioned their living room as a place where they could sit quietly and watch. "We couldn't imagine a greater experience," she says. "Our goal was to bring the outside in." Distance and intimacy mesh here; boundaries disappear. The living and dining room inserts itself right into the view: It's a box in the air—as Le Corbusier advised—but for these homeowners the experience isn't just a response to a set of modernist rules. It's personal, elevating their sense of wonder and even their well-being. Constraints have been lifted: "The house feels like it's floating in space," says the owner. "It feels that way inside, too." ●

↑ Wall-height windows on two sides of the house face directly into oncoming weather, fully immersing the owners in their surroundings.

← Precise geometry dominates this design. Scored poured-in-place concrete walls and walkways define the exterior walls.

← [preceding pages] Windows follow a strict hierarchy. On ground level, rectangular windows are punched into the concrete; above, steel-framed windows are set as a continuous band adjoining a projecting glazed element, which is replicated at the top of the house as a fully glazed wall.

← A black chimney punctuates the end of the house.

↓ An open-air lounge on the ground floor is an all-seasons venue for removing hiking gear, unbuckling snowshoes or skis, or just relaxing in the hot tub.

← [preceding pages] The house butts up against a hillside, which is an intense textural backdrop for the living room. A neutral palette of softly textured fabrics, light oak floors, and white plaster walls complements the colors of the landscape.

↑ The primary suite is in a glass-encased world of its own at the top of the house with views down to Maroon Creek and across to the Elk Mountains in the distance.

← Faceted porcelain forms by Mo Cornelisse are installed in the entry hall, catching light from the double-height window at the end of the space.

project credits

preserving the land
Architect: Gluck+, New York
Interior designer: Anne Kaplan, Insight Environmental Design, Highland Park, Illinois
Landscape architect: Joseph Wells Land Planning, Aspen

aspen meadows townhouse
Architects: Herbert Bayer/Fuse Architecture & Luis Mendez Architects, Aspen
Interior designer: Owner

along conundrum creek
Architect: Studio B Architecture + Interiors, Aspen
Interior designer: Chad James Group, Nashville
Landscape architect: Lift Studio, Aspen

a long view
Architect: Ellie Brickham/Rowland + Broughton Architecture and Interior Design, Aspen
Interior designer: Rowland + Broughton
Landscape architect: Bluegreen, Aspen

true west
Architect: Lake|Flato Architects, San Antonio
Interior designer: Collarte Interiors, Miami
Landscape architect: Bluegreen, Aspen

west end garden
Architect: S2 Architects, Aspen
Landscape architect: Elements, Aspen

a dream fulfilled
Architect: Oppenheim Architecture, Miami
Interior designer: Chad Oppenheim

modernist revival
Architect: Bohlin Cywinski Jackson, Wilkes Barre, Pennsylvania
Interior designer: SheltonMindel, New York
Landscape architect: Bluegreen, Aspen

in the valley
Architect: Eigelberger Architecture + Design, Aspen
Interior designer: Lindsay Henderson Interiors, Greensboro, North Carolina
Landscape architect: Design Workshop, Aspen

three trees
Architect: Gwathmey Siegel & Associates (now Gwathmey Siegel Kaufman), New York
Interior designer: Fox Nahem, New York

victorian music box
Architect: CCY Architects, Aspen
Interior designer: Cheryl Troxel Interiors, Santa Rosa Beach, Florida
Landscape architect: Bluegreen, Aspen

bayer redux
Architect: S2 Architects, Aspen
Interior designer: Owner
Landscape architect: Elements, Aspen

inviting the light
Architect: EYRC Architects, Los Angeles
Interior designer: Kristi Will Home & Design, Half Moon Bay, California
Landscape architect: Lift Studio, Aspen

classical modernism
Architect: Michael G. Imber Architects, San Antonio
Interior designer: Suzy Wheeler, Houston
Landscape architect: Owner

bayer legacy
Architect: Herbert Bayer/ Gilbert Sanchez, Aspen
Interior designer: Jackie Greenberg Interior Design, New York

building memories
Architect: CCY Architects, Aspen
Interior designer: Owner
Landscape architect: Mt. Daly Enterprises, Carbondale, Colorado

alpine influence
Architect: Rowland + Broughton Architecture and Interior Design, Aspen
Interior designer: Rowland + Broughton
Landscape architect: Land Design 39, Aspen

in the clouds
Architect: Zone 4 Architects, Aspen
Interior designer: Studio Piet Boon, Oostzaan, Netherlands
Landscape architect: Connect One Design, Basalt

acknowledgments

Private Aspen is the fourth in my series on modernist architecture. *Marfa Modern, Texas Made/Texas Modern*, and *Santa Fe Modern* were an opportunity to explore what has become an obsession: how modernism came to the American West and how, subsequently, it developed into true American architecture.

I would like to thank Elizabeth White at Monacelli for encouraging me in this pursuit and especially for presenting to me the idea of a book on Aspen modernist architecture. I have long been the beneficiary of her elegant editing and now have enjoyed her insights into more comprehensive aspects of creating books. This book, in particular, appealed because of the topic: Aspen is well known, sought after, and sometimes notorious.

But there is a part of Aspen's history that isn't so well known. Until now, no book has offered a view inside Aspen houses and demonstrated the town's emergence as a mecca for many of the world's greatest modernist architects. Most had fled Nazi Germany, and some found their way to Aspen. I show the legacy they left—both in the loving renovations to existing modernist houses and in new houses with a clear modernist provenance. Architecture here is the visual language that began as a message of freedom, invention, and imagination to the rest of the world exhausted by war.

There are wonderful books that capably describe Aspen's cultural development—*From Bauhaus to Aspen* by Gwen Chanzit; *Herbert Bayer Collection, An Archive at the Denver Art Museum*; and *One Hour Ahead: The Avant-Garde in Aspen, 1945–2004,* published by the Aspen Art Museum. My mission was to go beyond those narratives. Architecture has, since the mid-1950s, been the intentional language of Aspen, one that Aspen Institute founder and visionary Walter Paepcke chose as the way to express his hope for the future.

Telling the tale I found so compelling had its obstacles. As the title of the book makes clear, Aspen is a private town. Tucked into the Rockies and accessible seven months out of the year by only one road, Aspen is the ultimate redoubt. Here, leaders in finance, industry, technology, and the arts have found their retreat and expect to enjoy their privacy.

That fact alone makes me grateful to the eighteen homeowners (most wish to remain anonymous) who opened their houses to me. I am also grateful to the people who connected me to projects I needed to know about. Sheridan Mitchell Lorenz, Bill Harriman, John Sarpa, Lissa Ballinger, Ann Marie Koshuta, Steve Hansen, Scott Stricker, Mindy Pantiel, and John Wright Schaefer offered insights into the variety and complexity of architectural passions in Aspen.

Many thanks to photographer David Marlow who, besides excelling at his craft, was an invaluable guide to Aspen.

Thanks, too, to Laura Mintz, director of marketing and publicity at Monacelli, and Michael Vagnetti, production director, for the enthusiasm they have shown from the beginning.

Finally, special thanks to graphic designer Paco Lacasta for his appreciation of Bauhaus master Herbert Bayer's universal influence in the worlds of design, architecture, art, and ideas. Lacasta has gracefully incorporated a typeface that honors Bayer's legacy, and he has invigorated the graphic symbolism throughout the book, using the triangle, the circle, and the square shapes so meaningful to Bayer and to the Bauhaus movement. It is a pleasure to experience Lacasta's discerning inclusion of the Bauhaus design legacy throughout *Private Aspen*. By doing so, he invokes the startling extent to which the modernist dreamers made their impact.

Their ideas took hold and surely in no place more dramatic than Aspen. It represented a wild world that demanded originality and courage—ever the iconoclasts, modernist architects responded by building into the landscape, winding around it, or excavating under it. They anticipated a robust architecture that could only have emerged in the American West. I am grateful to have the opportunity to write about it.

First published in 2025

ISBN: 978-1-58093-656-9

Library of Congress Control Number: 2025936235

Editor: Elizabeth White
Production: Michael Vagnetti
Design: Lacasta Design

Printed in China

Phaidon Press Limited
2 Cooperage Yard
London E15 2QR

Monacelli
A Phaidon Company
111 Broadway
New York, NY 10006

Phaidon SARL
55, rue Traversière
75012 Paris

phaidon.com/monacelli

Photographs by David Marlow

Except as noted below:
William Abranowicz/Art + Commerce 176–77
Alamy 11 (left top and bottom), 14–15, 50–51, 62–63, 88–89, 112–13, 126–27, 138–39
Aspen Historical Society, Aspen Illustrated News Collection 8 (upper left)
Aspen Historical Society, Ringquist Collection 8 (upper right)
Brent Moss Boetcher 8 (below)
Shade Degges 64
Joe Fletcher 66–67, 162, 164, 165, 166–67
Bernard Jazzar 11 (lower right)
Brandon Huttenlocher 78–79, 100–101, 114, 116, 117, 118, 119, 120, 121, 122, 123, 124–25, 148–49, 160–61, 168–69, 182–83, 194–95, 208–9, 236–37
Steve Mundinger/GLUCK+ 22–23, 26, 27, 28–29
Post Company 12 (below)
Draper White 12 (top), 38–39, 40, 42–43, 44, 45, 46, 47, 48, 49, 144–45

Endpapers: Herbert Bayer, *Mountains and Lakes*, 1948. Lithograph. Courtesy of the Estate of Herbert Bayer, Jonathan Bayer, Miranda Bayer, KoKo Bayer, and Peyton Wright Gallery, Santa Fe